NEW VANGUARD • 163

BRITISH DESTROYERS 1892–1918

JIM CROSSLEY   ILLUSTRATED BY PAUL WRIGHT

First published in Great Britain in 2009 by Osprey Publishing,
Midland House, West Way, Botley, Oxford, OX2 0PH, UK
443 Park Avenue South, New York, NY 10016, USA
E-mail: info@ospreypublishing.com

A CIP catalog record for this book is available from the British Library

ISBN: 978 1 84603 514 2
E-book ISBN: 978 1 84908 119 1

Page layout by: Melissa Orrom Swan, Oxford
Index by Alan Thatcher
Typeset in Sabon and Myriad Pro
Originated by United Graphic Pte Ltd, Singapore
Printed in China through Worldprint Ltd.
09 10 11 12 13   10 9 8 7 6 5 4 3 2 1

FOR A CATALOGUE OF ALL BOOKS PUBLISHED BY OSPREY MILITARY
AND AVIATION PLEASE CONTACT:

Osprey Direct, c/o Random House Distribution Center,
400 Hahn Road, Westminster, MD 21157
Email: uscustomerservice@ospreypublishing.com

Osprey Direct, The Book Service Ltd, Distribution Centre,
Colchester Road, Frating Green, Colchester, Essex, CO7 7DW
E-mail: customerservice@ospreypublishing.com

www.ospreypublishing.com

Osprey Publishing is supporting the Woodland Trust, the UK's leading
woodland conservation charity, by funding the dedication of trees.

EDITOR'S NOTE

For ease of comparison between types, imperial measurements are
used almost exclusively throughout this book. The following details
will help in converting the imperial measurements into metric:

1 mile = 1.6km
1lb = 0.45kg
1 yard = 0.9m
1ft = 0.3m
1in = 2.54cm/25.4mm
1 gal = 4.5 liters
1 ton (US) = 0.9 tonnes

CONTENTS

BRITISH DESTROYERS 1892–1918

INTRODUCTION: THE TORPEDO MENACE

Warships evolved at an astonishing pace in the second half of the 19th century. Wooden sailing ships firing smoothbore cannon gave way to armoured steamships with turret-mounted, rifled, long-range guns. Through the course of this development Britain, while not the originator of every innovation, was invariably able to maintain a substantial margin of superiority over any other power. One weapon, however, seemed to threaten to negate its superiority in capital ships. The self-propelled torpedo, invented by Whitehead in the 1860s and coming into general use in the 1870s and 1880s, seemed to offer the prospect of a weapon that could allow a small torpedo-boat to inflict serious damage on the most powerful warship. British admirals fretted about the prospect of fleets of small French vessels creeping up at night, or in foggy weather, on Portsmouth, Plymouth or Portland and eliminating the nation's protective shield at a stroke. By the mid-1880s most of the major naval powers had built fleets of small wooden torpedo-boats of about 100-ton displacement each and capable of 20 knots or so in calm water with about 1,000hp.

Some naval strategists predicted the end of the armoured capital ship altogether. Especially vociferous in this regard was the so-called *Jeune École* ("Young School") – an influential group of French naval officers. Their arguments were fortified by two events. One was the successful use of torpedo-boats by the Imperial Russian Navy, which had launched primitive self-propelled torpedoes against a Turkish squadron in 1878, and succeeded in sinking a small gunboat. The second event was more significant. In August 1884 a French squadron under Admiral Amédée Courbert used two small torpedo-boats with devastating effect while inflicting a crushing defeat on a much more numerous Chinese force at Foochow.

Among measures taken to address the menace of the torpedo was a class of "torpedo-boat catchers", armed with the newly developed quick-firing guns, which were intended to catch and destroy would-be attackers before they reached their targets. It then occurred to ship designers that these catchers could themselves be torpedo-armed and thus acquire an offensive as well as a defensive role. A number of attempts to achieve this were made in the 1880s and early 1890s, including the Royal Navy's Rattlesnake and Gossamer (or Sharpshooter) classes. All of these vessels were of very conventional design, typically about 550 to 800 tons in displacement and 200 to 250ft long. However, they were to prove totally inadequate for their intended task. Their maximum speed of up to 19kt was less than that of the

boats they were supposed to catch, and in any case they were far too big with too deep a draught for their intended purpose. Although 39 of these boats were built, all were rapidly relegated to other duties.

THE FIRST TORPEDO-BOAT DESTROYERS

The British Admiralty, under the energetic and innovative leadership of Admiral Jackie Fisher, then decided that a far more radical approach to the problem was required. In an uncharacteristic delegation of responsibilities, instead of designing the new class of ship itself, the Admiralty provided civilian builders capable of delivering fast small craft with an outline specification of what was required and allowed them to come up with their own way of achieving it. The Admiralty reserved the right to reject any design it deemed unseaworthy or otherwise unsatisfactory. It also introduced a system of "payment by results" whereby a design falling slightly below the specified speed would be accepted, but at a reduced price, and sometimes a premium would be paid to a builder whose product surpassed the specification. This system was retained for all the early classes of British destroyer, so they all differed according to builder even when they were built to the same specification. Eventually more than a dozen builder/designers were to become involved. Many of these were originally based on the Thames but moved their operations elsewhere as labour rates close to London became uncompetitive.

The Royal Navy continued to call these vessels TBDs until 1919, but the term "destroyer" was in common parlance and was eventually adopted officially. This will be the term used throughout this narrative.

Grasshopper, launched in 1887, was an early attempt at a torpedo gunboat but was totally unsuitable for the task, having a top speed of only 17kt. It was armed with 14in torpedoes and one 4in gun. *Grasshopper* was scrapped in 1905.

Havoc, launched in 1893, was the first true TBD. It could make 26kt in smooth water. The closely set funnels indicate that the vessel had locomotive-type boilers. The man standing behind the 12-pounder gives an idea of how exposed this position would be in a seaway. The conning tower is underneath the gun platform. Note the bow torpedo tube.

The specifications provided to the first builders in 1892 were radical. These were to be the fastest warships afloat, yet were supposed to be able to stay at sea in any weather. They were to be fast enough and well enough armed to run down and destroy the latest French Normand Class torpedo-boats, yet be able to carry an offensive load of torpedoes themselves, capable of disabling any battleship.

Maximum speed was to be 27kt when armed with one bow torpedo, one 12-pounder gun, three six-pounders, and either two additional six-pounders or two revolving torpedo tubes. Provision had to be made for two spare torpedoes. There had to be accommodation for a crew of 40 officers and men and storage for 40–50 tons of coal. Watertight bulkheads were to be provided so as to improve survivability in combat. Boats had to be delivered complete with electric lighting, one 24ft whaler and two 20ft Berthon folding boats. Initially two prototypes were ordered from each of two contractors, Yarrow and Thorneycroft, with two more ordered a little later from Laird.

Each prototype had two triple-expansion piston engines each developing about 2,000hp. They were typically 200ft long and 19ft wide with a draught of 7ft, which on some boats could be reduced by raising the screws. Displacement was a little over 270 tons, fully equipped. All these dimensions varied slightly between builders. In order to save weight the boats adopted a "stressed-skin" structural design comprising a quite light framework onto which were riveted thin steel plates. The vessels were totally unarmoured apart from the conning tower, and even that would only keep out small-arms fire or splinters.

There was intense debate over which type of boiler should be used – either a locomotive type, in which the hot gases passed from the firebox through tubes surrounded by boiler water, or the water-tube type with water circulating directly through tubes passing through the furnace. Both types were fitted on various prototypes, but eventually the locomotive type was abandoned.

The Yarrow-built boats HMS *Havelock* and HMS *Hornet* were laid down in July 1892 and completed in August and December of the following year at a cost of just over £36,000 each. Thorneycroft took about three months longer to build its two prototypes, HMS *Daring* and HMS *Decoy*, for a very similar price. The Thorneycroft-built boats were slightly heavier (287.8 tons

Daring, one of the Thorneycroft-built A Class boats. It had water-tube boilers.

fully loaded against 275 tons) and were generally considered to be rather better built. Laird's two prototypes, HMS *Ferret* and HMS *Lynx*, appeared a little later and were similar in terms of size and cost.

All six prototypes were accepted into service and proved that this entirely new class of vessel was not only practical but also represented an extremely potent new weapon of naval warfare. It is immensely to the credit of both the Navy and its chosen constructors that some of the boats from the very earliest batch of destroyers were still in service in 1918.

DESIGN AND CONSTRUCTION

The early destroyers were distinguished by their long, narrow hulls (the length–to–beam ratio being greater than 10 : 1), almost two-thirds of which were taken up by boilers and machinery. The single bow torpedo-tube was placed under the "turtleback" foredeck, where there was space for stowing the two spare torpedoes Also in the bow section were seamen's berths and ammunition storage. The turtleback was common to all builders' designs and was intended to improve buoyancy forward. It was often completely submerged in rough weather. The bow torpedo-tube proved useless in practice as it could only be operated in smooth water and its blunt shape in the bow of the boat caused problems with spray being thrown aft onto the gun and conning tower. Bow tubes were abandoned in later vessels.

The 12-pounder quick-firing gun was mounted on a platform above the conning tower. The gunner's platform, which was also used by the officer conning the ship in action, consisted of timber slats which allowed cold air and spray to surge up vertically underneath anyone on the platform. This, combined with the lack of any windscreen and the clouds of spray thrown up when steaming at speed, made the position extremely wet and uncomfortable. It would have been impossible to use the gun when the boat was moving fast, or in bad weather. The practice when chasing torpedo-boats was to pursue an enemy to about 500yd range, then stop to fire.

The conning tower was a small structure, protected by half-inch steel plate. There was one outside and one inside steering position. This arrangement was one of the least successful features of the design: the outside position was untenable in rough weather, being swamped in spray, and the inside position allowed only very restricted vision through small portholes in the armour plating. Damp and vibration made the compass extremely difficult to read. Aft of the conning tower were the two Hotchkiss six-pounder quick-firers and the forward forced-draught engine air intake. Beneath this a large fan was used to create high air pressure in the engine room so as to improve the draught in the furnaces. There was a further intake and fan at the aft end of the boiler room. All destroyers had at least one mast located aft of the conning tower with crosstrees for hoisting signal flags, and some of the earliest boats were actually provided with sails to steady them in rough weather. Radio was not fitted until the early 1900s, at which time the mast was modified and used to carry the aerial. Due to the many different types of boilers fitted the number and position of funnels varied widely. Locomotive boilers placed end-to-end allowed a single funnel or two close together, whereas boats with water-tube boilers would normally have four widely spaced funnels. It soon became apparent that on the prototypes the funnels were too short, allowing flare from the furnaces to give away the boat's position in the dark. Subsequently, taller funnels were fitted. Below the funnels were the boilers and stokehold and behind these were the boats and davits.

Aft of the stokehold were the engines. Early boats were fitted with two triple-expansion units, in most cases designed and built by the same yard as the boats themselves. They drove two shafts at up to about 400rpm. An excellent contemporary description exists of conditions in the boiler room of an early destroyer:

> Observe the chargeman in the stokehold with his hand on the fan regulator, his eye on the gauges, his foot among the coals. He inspects the fires through his coloured glasses and directs the fireman who visits each furnace with increasing regularity, spreading shovel loads evenly over the fires...the triple beat of the engines merges into a prolonged roar, occasionally assuming a distinct period as the two engines get into step; this is felt through the whole ship, the stern in particular appearing to jump violently up and down...dust obscures the gauges and telegraphs: dust gets into the fan engines, which promptly run hot and require water to cool them. The water descends on the bare heads of the firemen.

In these conditions a team of six stokers would have to deliver five to seven tons of coal an hour to the furnaces when running at full speed. Stokers worked in shifts typically two hours in duration. Further aft, in the engine room, conditions were no better. Men would be playing hoses on bearing surfaces to keep them cool and spraying oil onto moving parts, all in an inferno of noise and heat and an atmosphere laden with oil vapour and coal dust. Stokers and engine-room crews would be working at the limit of human endurance.

Above the engine room was the searchlight and behind them twin torpedo tubes mounted on a turntable and arranged head to tail; this arrangement constituted the vessel's main armament. During the lifetime of these ships, torpedoes developed rapidly. At the time the ships were constructed maximum range was about 500yd at 40kt, but in practice the chances of hitting anything but a large stationary target at anything like 500yd were extremely slim. Fourteen-inch torpedoes were originally specified, but these were changed to 18in early in the life of these boats. Behind the tubes was a further Hotchkiss six-pounder. Aft of this a windscreen protected the after steering position.

In practice this steering position was found to be very difficult to use due to the poor view and the length of the vessel. The wardroom and officers' accommodation were located aft, beneath the six-pounder.

The propellers and rudder protruded beyond the dimensions of the hull itself, the propellers being protected by tubular steel guardrails. Cooking and accommodation arrangements were rudimentary, as the boats were not intended to stay at sea for long periods. Crews slept and ate ashore when in port. Nevertheless, life on destroyers was considered exceptionally tough and crews received a special "hard-lying allowance" in consideration of this. As time went on destroyer crews developed an ethos of their own, very different from that of the highly disciplined and regimented atmosphere of the rest of the Navy. On the whole they were happy ships on which officers and men worked well together.

Tests of the six prototypes led the Admiralty to order a further 36 boats from 14 different builders. The boats were of similar design but without the bow torpedo-tubes and with slightly longer funnels to reduce emission of sparks and glare from the furnaces. These vessels were collectively known as the "A Class". In service they proved astonishingly durable, many of them serving throughout World War I, often in a minesweeping role. Two of them, *Boxer* and *Decoy*, were lost in 1918 after colliding and one, *Lightning*, was sunk by a mine. The rest all seem to have survived the war, and been broken up. There was some concern about their structural integrity, especially on stations where severe weather was common. At one stage extensive repair was not considered worthwhile beyond a finite life of five or ten years, because the hulls were so light, but clearly this was not accepted as some boats served for more than 20 years.

TBDS ENTER SERVICE

Despite their revolutionary design and narrow beam the early TBDs proved to be reasonable sea boats, not one of them being wrecked due to stress of

The C Class destroyer *Albatross*. These 30kt ships were all fairly similar. Most survived to take part in World War I, often in an ancillary or minesweeping role. Note that the bow torpedo tube is gone but the conning tower is still underneath the gun platform.

weather. It became apparent in service the nominal speed of 27kt could hardly ever be approached. This was partly because the boats were often overloaded with all sorts of extra equipment, and partly because crews knew that running at full speed was sure to result in premature engine breakdown. Stoker exhaustion also limited the potential for sustained high speeds. In anything like bad weather it was a question of forgetting about making progress and adopting survival mode. Best practice in such circumstances was to power slowly ahead with the bows pointing about 15 degrees off the wind, keeping all hands safely below. It was essential to ensure that all openings on deck were firmly secured or the vessel would flood. In any event water would get in through the vents and down the funnels. The turtleback bow would bury itself in the oncoming waves and the boat would virtually "submarine" through them. It is difficult to imagine what it must have been like working in the stokehold. Seasickness was a constant problem, and officers and men who could not tolerate the sustained violent motion experienced in destroyers were rapidly posted elsewhere.

Before the last of the A Class were completed the Admiralty undertook construction of a larger class of destroyers, known as the B Class or "Thirty-Knotters". These entered service between 1896 and 1908. They were more standardised than the A Class, and were all fitted with water-tube boilers and had four funnels. They also had three propeller shafts instead of two as on the older vessels. Although their tonnage was 30 per cent greater than their predecessors', they had the same armament, the extra weight deriving from the engines (rated at 6,000hp instead of 4,000hp) and the amount of coal carried. Like the A Class ships they very rarely achieved their design speed in practice.

Almost simultaneously, orders for two further distinct classes were set in hand. The C Class was similar in size and power to the B Class but more heavily armed, with five six-pounders instead of three as well as the usual 12-pounder. The torpedo tubes were on two independent turntables arranged in tandem. These ships had three funnels and two propellers. A variation on the same theme was the Thorneycroft-designed D Class. These ships represented a real step forward: built of high-tensile steel, they were slightly lighter and stronger than B- and C-class vessels. A total of 58 B, C and D class destroyers were built, although not all entered service for various reasons. Seven of them, *Lightning*, *Cheerful*, *Fairy*, *Flirt*, *Recruit*, *Coquette* and *Velox* were sunk by enemy action during the war, mostly falling victim to mines. Four were wrecked in various circumstances and three were lost in collisions.

Many of these early boats were deployed on distant stations, including China, the West Indies, Malta, the Cape of Good Hope, and the Pacific. The ships' level of seaworthiness was attested to by their safe arrival at these destinations, although it was normally felt prudent for TBDs to travel in company with a cruiser. In service many of them had to be strengthened, especially in the bow section where the plates could become distorted by heavy pounding. Engine reliability was a constant problem in service, with many letters of complaint on that score on file. However, to be fair to the builders, all piston engines on warships suffered from frequent breakdowns if they were run at high speed for any length of time. Attempts were made to compare the quality of boats from the different builders. No firm conclusions were reached, but most people considered the Palmer-built boats to be the best and the Laird-built the worst in terms of reliability. Palmer and Hawthorn Leslie-built vessels were considered the best sea boats.

SPECIFICATIONS

General specifications

These three early TBD classes were far from homogeneous, so outline specifications are given below.

	A Class	B Class	C and D classes
Displacement:	260 tons	355–470 tons	355 tons
Length:	200ft	210ft	210ft
Beam:	19ft	21ft	21ft
Draught:	7ft	5.5ft	9ft
Gun armament:	One 12pdr, five 6pdr	One 12pdr, five 6pdr	One 12pdr, five 6pdr
Torpedoes:	Two 14in	Two 18in	Two 18in
Power:	4,000hp	6,000hp	6,000hp
Speed:	27kt	30kt	30kt

Note: D Class boats were slightly less powerful and had shallower draught.

Turbines

The Parsons turbine engine was a vast improvement on the triple-expansion units fitted in all the early destroyers because it had a far better power-to-weight ratio, created much less vibration and was potentially infinitely more reliable. However, early turbine engines did have some severe drawbacks. These included inability to run in reverse, very high fuel consumption at cruising speeds, and the fact that the high rotational speeds of turbine shafts made it extremely difficult to arrive at an efficient arrangement of propellers. Early experience with turbine-engined destroyers seemed to confirm doubts about their suitability.

The first turbine-engined destroyer was *Viper*, built by Hawthorn Leslie under contract to Parsons and launched in 1899. This was basically a C Class boat, and had four shafts, on each of which was two small-diameter propellers. Two separate turbines drove the two inner shafts when going astern. In trials *Viper* proved to be the fastest ship in the world, achieving just under 34kt, but it soon became apparent that any attempt to sustain this sort of speed was restricted by the number of stokers available. No fewer than 32 were needed to achieve maximum speed, and there was not anything like enough space

Viper, the first turbine-powered TDB. Although very fast it was not a success due to its voracious appetite for coal, even when cruising at low speeds. It was eventually wrecked off the Channel Islands.

A **HORNET**

Hornet was one of the first batch of TDBs ordered by the Royal Navy from Yarrows. She was completed in 1893 and along with her sister *Havoc* were the first viable TBDs. She was fitted with water tube boilers, which eventually proved superior to the locomotive type boilers used on *Havoc*. The arrangement of the boilers dictated the number of funnels, *Hornet* had four and *Havoc* two. Accommodation was provided for 40 officers and men, but they must have been extremely cramped and in fact they were accommodated ashore when the ship was in port. Note how the bow torpedo tube breaks the fine line of the bows and resulted in the ship being extremely wet in a seaway. Another unsatisfactory feature was the armoured conning tower visible beneath the 12-pounder gun. Visibility for the helmsman was very bad. Note the "A" frame supporting the propellers, and the guard rail to prevent them being damaged when coming alongside. She achieved a fraction under 27 kt on trials and carried 60 tons of coal. Her service life was spent in home waters. These first TBDs, especially the Yarrow boats, were slightly too frail for a long service life and soon became uneconomic to repair. *Hornet* was sold and broken up in 1909.

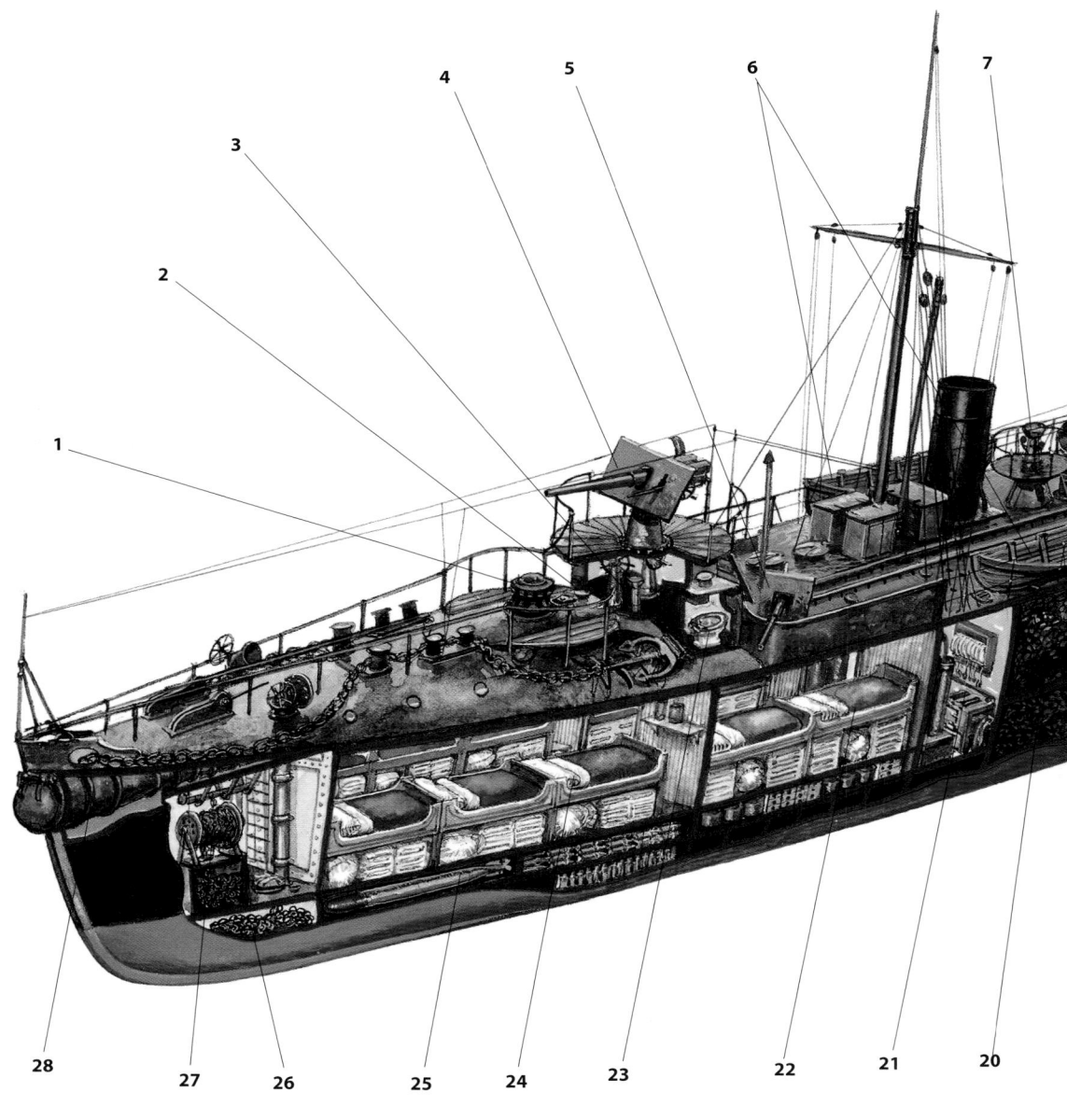

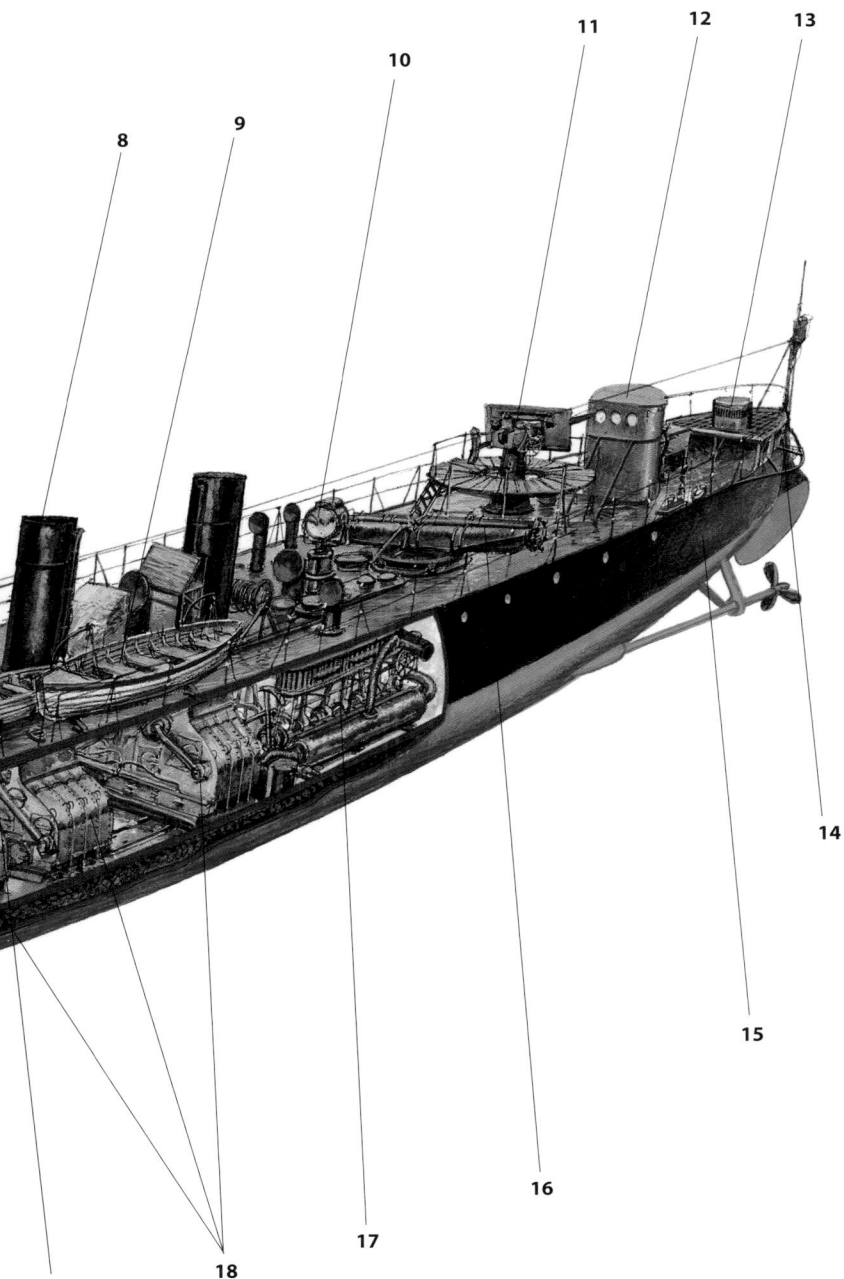

aboard to accommodate this number in service. *Viper* was wrecked off Alderney early in its career. The other early turbine destroyer, *Cobra*, was also based on the C Class design, but was slightly larger (displacing 375 tons as opposed to 344 tons), mainly because it carried 20 tons more coal. However, the ship was not a success – it broke in two soon after trials, possibly due to extra weight of coal combined with inadequate hull design. A comparison between *Viper* and another C Class piston-engined boat, *Albatross*, illustrates the problem of fuel consumption with turbines (see table below).

At full speed there is little to choose between them, but for cruising the turbine's performance was clearly unacceptable. It was nevertheless obvious that to achieve sustained speeds of more than 30kt piston engines were operating outside their proper limits, as witnessed by their very poor reliability record. The Admiralty therefore determined to press on with experiments with turbines.

	Speed	Coal consumption	Nautical miles per ton	Bunkerage	Range*
Viper	31kt	8.8 tons/hr	3.51	86 tons	300
	15kt	1.3 tons/hr	11	86 tons	920
Albatross	31kt	7.6 tons/hr	4	104 tons	410
	14.3kt	0.6 tons/hr	22.6	104 tons	2,200

* Range in nautical miles allowing for auxiliary uses.

The next turbine boat was *Velox*, built in 1904 by Hawthorn Leslie under contract to Parsons. The hull form was basically that of a C Class boat. This time two separate piston engines of 150hp each were provided for cruising. Again, the results were disappointing. At maximum speed fully loaded it consumed almost ten tons of coal per hour and even at cruising speed using the piston engines *Velox's* economy was poor. However, it was retained in service, finally being scrapped in 1915 after striking a mine.

The final attempt at powering these early boats with turbines occurred in 1909 with the construction of *Albacore* and *Bonetta*. Actually modified B Class boats, they were built by the firm of Palmer to replace two destroyers, *Tiger* and *Gala*, which had been lost in April 1908. The latest boats had some interesting new features, including a finer bow and a longer foredeck than other B Class boats, and a full-width bridge instead of the unsatisfactory

Cygnet was a D Class TBD built by Thorneycroft using high-tensile steel. D Class boats were very similar to those of the A and B classes, but significantly faster due to lighter construction. They achieved more than 30kt in still water.

conning-tower arrangement. They carried two 12-pounders in addition to the usual complement of six-pounders and torpedoes. However, they proved disappointing in terms of speed, for which the builder paid a heavy penalty. Both boats survived the war and were broken up in 1919 and 1920.

In reality, turbines still had severe limitations when applied to these small vessels. The very small propellers rotating at high speed were inevitably inefficient, and only with the advent of geared turbines was this overcome. In addition, the voracious appetite for fuel displayed by these high-powered engines was impossible for a destroyer's small crew to satisfy for any length of time. This was a problem which could only be overcome by the advent of oil.

THE SHIPS: EARLY DEVELOPMENTS

River Class

The A, B, C and D Class boats successfully demonstrated that fast small vessels could hunt down enemy torpedo boats in any weather – which was after all their primary role – and that they could deliver torpedoes in suitable circumstances. However, new developments meant a somewhat different approach was called for. The most important of these innovations was a marked improvement in the range, speed and stability of torpedoes. In the 1880s and 1890s the concept had been that torpedo-firing boats should sneak up to enemy ships in harbour or at anchor and launch surprise attacks at short range. In the early 1900s a new generation of 18in torpedoes came into service that incorporated the improved Brotherhood engine and used steam heating and gyroscopic directional control. The weapons' effective range and destructive power increased so dramatically that they were now considered suitable for use by the battlefleet at sea. By 1914 most destroyers in service were armed with 18in or later 21in torpedoes with a range of 3,800yd at 45kt and 10,000yd at 28kt (although, as history would show, the chances of hitting a moving ship in battle conditions at anything like these ranges was extremely remote). The use of such weapons might have a dramatic effect on a sea battle. There was therefore demand for a new type of torpedo-armed destroyer, large enough and seaworthy enough to operate with the fleet in all weathers. Germany, which was rapidly developing its naval strength at this time, pre-empted the British by launching *S90*, a 350-ton destroyer with greatly enhanced seakeeping qualities, in 1900.

The Royal Navy's answer to this was the E or River Class destroyers, of which 39 were built between 1903 and 1905. The E Class ships were quite

The E or River Class destroyer *Arun*. Note the bridge located behind the 12-pounder gun and the raised forecastle, giving much improved performance in rough weather. However, these ships were 5kt slower in still water than boats of the C Class.

unlike their predecessors in having a raised forecastle instead of a turtleback and a proper bridge structure in place of a conning tower. They were also much bigger vessels with a broader beam and slightly deeper draught. Most River Class vessels were powered by triple-expansion engines, and all were coal-fired. However, three – *Eden*, *Stour* and *Test* – were turbine-powered. With only 7,000hp the River Class ships were inevitably slower than all previous destroyers in still water, with a maximum speed of only 25kt, but in anything like a seaway they were far more capable than the earlier TBDs. The higher forecastle allowed the forward guns to be operated even when steaming into a head sea. Two separate torpedo tubes were mounted, one between the funnels and one aft. Some early ships were fitted with the same armament as the C Class, but this was soon changed to four twelve-pounders. Although still officially termed "torpedo-boat destroyers" by the Admiralty, these were in truth "ships" rather than "boats", and will be referred to as "ships" in this narrative.

River Class ships were constructed by six of the established destroyer builders and were different from each other in appearance, some having two funnels and some having four in two pairs, this arrangement being dictated by boiler type.

A comparison with the C Class is instructive (see table below).

	C Class	River Class
Displacement:	355 tons	550 tons
Length:	210ft	225ft
Beam:	21ft	23ft 6in
Draught:	9ft	10ft
Armament:	One 12pdr Five 6pdr Two 18in torpedoes	Four 12pdr Two 18in torpedoes
Machinery:	6,000hp	7,000hp
Maximum speed:	30kt	25kt
Fuel:	80 tons	120 tons

VELOX AND RIVER CLASS

Velox (1)

This C Class destroyer was built by Hawthorn under contract to Parsons in 1902. It was one of the first turbine-engined TBDs. It had four shafts and eight screws rotating at high speed and directly driven by the turbines. Note that a searchlight is fitted and the bow tube has been deleted from the design; instead, two rotating single tubes are fitted aft of the funnels. However, there is no improvement in visibility from the conning tower. *Velox* is much more heavily armed than *Havoc*, having five six-pounders and one 12-pounder. Although very fast, with speed often exceeding 30kt, high fuel consumption made this destroyer unsatisfactory. *Velox* was mined on 25 October 1915 off the Nab Tower in the eastern approaches to the Solent.

River Class (2)

E or River Class destroyers were designed to be much better sea boats than the early TBDs. Note the raised forecastle in place of the turtleback. Also significant was the provision of a proper bridge in place of the conning tower. Too slow to work effectively with the battlefleet, these ships were extensively used for coastal patrols and minesweeping. Pictured here is *Chelmer*, launched by Thorneycroft in 1904. Appearance of River Class ships differed widely, some having two and some four funnels.

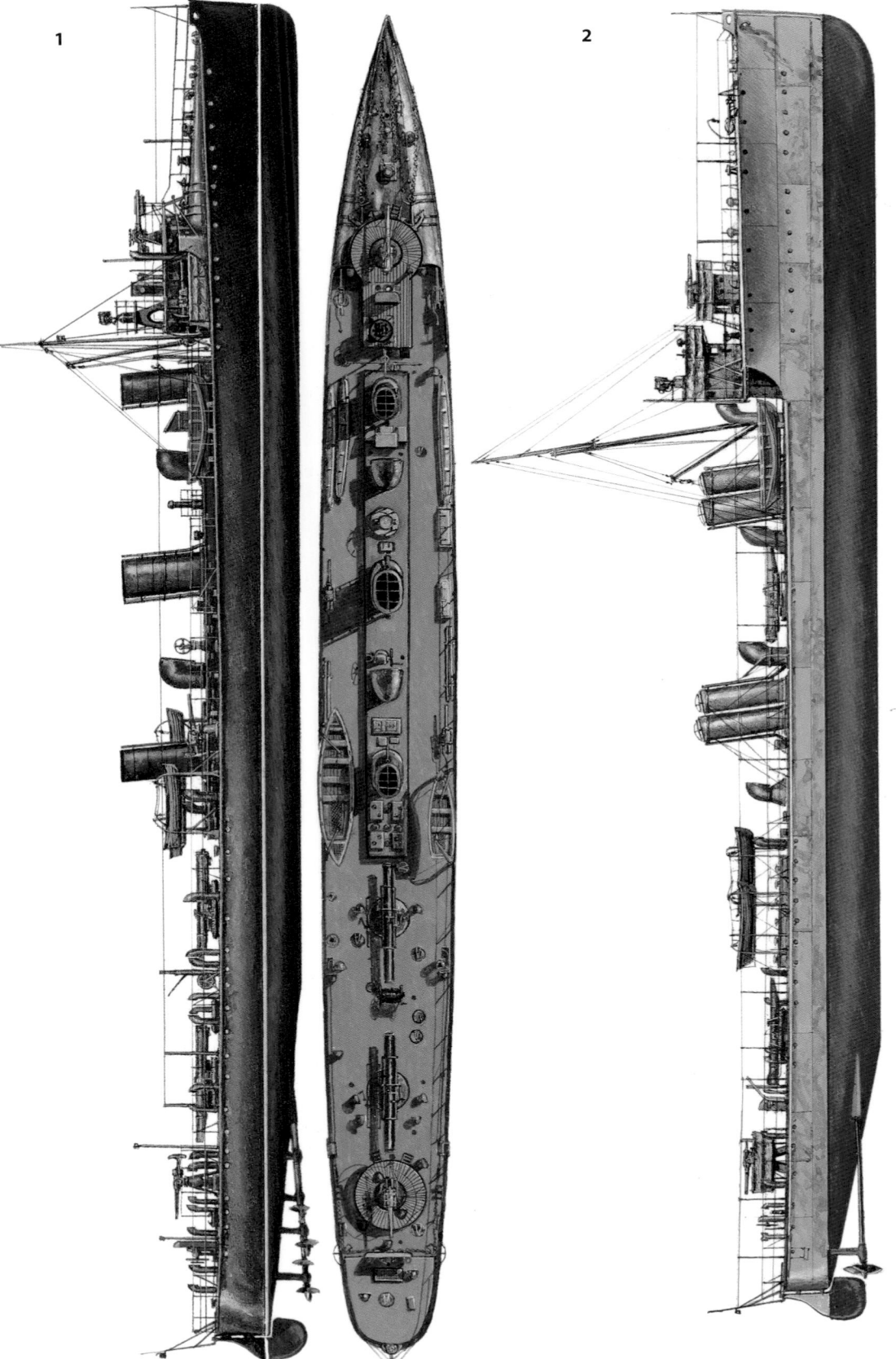

Mohawk, launched in 1907, was one of the early Tribal Class destroyers. These were considerably different from each other in appearance, some having three and some up to six funnels. They were powered by 14,000–15,500hp oil-fired turbines and were by some margin the fastest warships in the world when they were launched, some achieving well over 36kt. They were also heavily armed, with five 12-pounders or two 4in guns. In performance and armament they set an entirely new standard for destroyer fleets. During World War I they were mainly used as part of the Dover Patrol.

Five River Class destroyers were lost in the war, *Derwent*, *Foyle* and *Kale* being mined, and *Itchen* torpedoed by a U-boat, while *Eden* collided with SS *France* in the English Channel.

Tribal Class

By 1905 the revolutionary battleship *Dreadnought*, which was to be capable of 21kt, was on the stocks. It was joined later in the year by the 25kt battlecruiser *Indomitable*. If future destroyers were to work as effective scouts for these ships they clearly had to be much faster than destroyers of the River Class. The Navy was going to have to take the plunge and convert to turbine power and oil-firing.

The construction of 12 destroyers of the "F" or "Tribal" Class commenced in 1907. These magnificent ships formed an important part of the destroyer force throughout World War I. Each was slightly different from its fellows, later ships being generally bigger than early ones. They had anything from four to six funnels, depending on boiler type and configuration. Armament also varied, some having two 4in (25-pounder) guns and some five 12-pounders. All ships had two 18in torpedo tubes. They were much bigger than the ships of the River Class, with more than twice the horsepower.

In their day, the Tribal Class destroyers were the fastest ships afloat, and by some way. *Tartar*, for example, achieved 35.6kt in trials. Additionally, because they were oil-burning and had reliable turbine engines, they could and did maintain maximum speed for long periods with only a small crew.

Main dimensions are given in the table below.

Displacement:	870–970 tons
Length:	250–290ft
Beam:	26ft
Draught:	9ft
Armament:	Five 12pdr or two 4in guns, two 18in torpedo tubes
Machinery:	14,000–15,500hp
Maximum speed:	35kt
Fuel:	80–100 tons oil

In performance and armament these ships more or less set the standard for future generations of British destroyer. In addition to their revolutionary fuel and engine arrangements, the Tribal Class destroyers were the first to be fitted with radio, hence the tall foremast and short mast aft. However, they should not be confused with the much later generation of "Tribal Class" ships built in the 1930s, which gave excellent service in World War II. During the 1914–18 war *Gurkha*, *Maori* and *Zulu* were mined and *Nubian* was torpedoed. Astonishingly, the fore part of *Zulu* and the after part of *Nubian* were salvaged and then cobbled together to form a new vessel imaginatively named *Zubian*. Even more astonishingly, the hybrid was successful, going on to sink UC-50 by ramming in the North Sea in February 1918. The main drawback of the Tribal Class ships was their rather high cost; the Admiralty countered this by producing the "G" class described below, as well as a new class of coastal torpedo boats used for inshore work and boom defence.

THE SHIPS: SUBSEQUENT DEVELOPMENTS

The later generations of destroyer, described below, followed the course so often set by various types of warship. They steadily grew in size and gained in offensive armament, the latter consisting first of the new generation of 21in torpedoes and then the three or four 4in guns, which became the wartime standard. Later, as airpower began to play a part in naval warfare, some rudimentary anti-aircraft armament began to appear. More efficient engines with geared turbines and consequently larger-diameter propellers came into use, although these did not significantly improve on the maximum speed

Swift was a most formidable ship, eventually fitted with a 6in gun and 21in torpedoes. It was the first purpose-built flotilla leader, and was not approached in size by any British destroyer until 1937. It was also extremely fast, capable of 36kt. The 6in gun, the heaviest ever fitted to a British destroyer, is plainly visible on the foredeck.

established by the Tribal Class. By 1918 destroyers had evolved into considerably and larger more capable ships tasked with establishing and maintaining command of the North Sea, the English Channel and the Western Approaches. They were produced in very large numbers by Britain and its allies, particularly the USA.

Swift

Also in 1907 the Admiralty commissioned a "one-off" large destroyer designated as a flotilla leader. Its role was to accommodate a senior officer and his staff who would lead a flotilla of destroyers into action. This was a task that typically fell to light cruisers, but these were quite unsuitable for the role, being almost 10kt slower than turbine-engined destroyers. Ideally, a destroyer leader should have been larger than and at least as fast and heavily armed as the destroyers in its flotilla.

The first specialised flotilla leader, named *Swift*, was built with two 4in guns on the foredeck, but this armament was later converted to a single six-incher; in fact, *Swift* was the only British destroyer ever to carry such a big gun. Torpedo armament was also uprated and *Swift* became the first destroyer fitted with 21in in place of 18in tubes. With 30,000hp it was indeed formidable. It was also formidably expensive – at more than £250,000 costing seven times as much as an early destroyer.

Swift served successfully for most of the war with the Dover Patrol. The vessel's dimensions, given below, were not exceeded by other British destroyers until the 1930s.

Swift	
Displacement:	1,825 tons
Length:	353ft
Beam:	34ft 6in
Draught:	10ft 6in
Armament:	Earlier: Four 4in guns, two 18in torpedoes
	Later: One 6in gun, two 4in guns, two 21in torpedoes
Machinery:	30,000hp
Speed:	36kt
Fuel:	180 tons oil

C **TRIBAL AND M CLASS**

Tribal Class (1)

Tribal Class destroyers introduced turbines and oil burning. They were much the fastest warships in existence but their rather limited range made them unsuitable for work with the fleet. They were invaluable to the Dover Patrol. Some had two 4in guns. *Mohawk*, shown here, was built by the firm of White and was initially fitted with three 12-pounders and two 18in torpedo tubes. Note the smaller-diameter high-speed propellers dictated by the use of ungeared turbine engines.

M Class (2)

This class of vessel formed the backbone of the destroyer fleet from 1915 onward. Pictured is a typical Admiralty-design ship; different builders produced slight variants. These were excellent ships, and 110 were built between 1914 and 1917.

THE SHIPS: FURTHER DEVELOPMENTS

From 1907 onwards the Royal Navy recognised three types of destroyer:

Coastal destroyers: Relatively slow and low-cost.

Fleet destroyers: Fast ships able to operate with the battlefleet.

Flotilla leaders: Large, fast destroyers with accommodation for the flotilla commander.

The following tables give a summary of the G–W classes, completed up to 1918. Note that from the L Class onwards, all destroyer names began with the same letter as their class designation. Occasionally the Admiralty ran out of names, in which case the next letter was applied. For example, 112 M Class ships were built, the later ones having names beginning with N, O and P.

G Class

Displacement:	860–940 tons
Length:	275ft
Beam:	28ft
Draught:	8.5ft
Armament:	Earlier: One 4in gun, three 12pdr guns, two 18in torpedoes
	Later: Two 21in torpedoes
Machinery:	12,500hp
Speed:	27kt

These ships were developed in response to the new generation of German destroyers, the S13–S24 Class mounting two 4.1in guns, the plans of which the Admiralty had acquired. All G Class ships had three funnels. The 4in gun was mounted on a shelter deck so that it could be used in short, steep seas,

Harpy, shown in a heavy sea. This was a G Class ship intended for coastal defence and one of the last coal burners. Although almost 10kt slower than the Tribal Class vessels, these ships were more seaworthy, having the 4in gun mounted high up on a shelter-deck and a better-protected bridge. They were the first destroyers (apart from *Swift*) to carry 21in torpedoes.

and the bridge was higher than on the Tribal Class vessels, also with a view to improving seaworthiness. Designated as coastal ships, G Class destroyers were relatively slow. One torpedo tube was placed forward of the mainmast, the other on the stern. Turbines developed 12,500hp. In addition to their coastal destroyer role many were deployed to work with the light cruisers of the Harwich force and fought some spirited engagements in the North Sea and the Heligoland Bight.

Two were shipwrecked – *Pincher* on the Seven Stones off Land's End and *Racoon* off the Irish coast – and *Wolverine* was lost in a collision.

H Class

Displacement:	730–780 tons
Length:	246.5ft
Beam:	25.5ft
Draught:	7–10ft
Armament:	Two 4in guns, two 12pdr guns, one 3pdr AA gun, two 21in torpedoes
Machinery:	13,500hp
Speed:	27kt

The H Class were distinguished from the G Class by having a tall funnel forward and two shorter ones aft. The forward torpedo tube was placed between the two after funnels. The most important development was the two 4in turrets in "A" and "Y" positions; these were supplemented by two 12-pounders as secondary armament.

Comet and *Staunch* were torpedoed by U-boats in the Mediterranean, in separate incidents. *Goldfinch* was wrecked off the island of Sanday in Orkney. *Minstrel* and *Nemesis* were transferred to the Imperial Japanese Navy and renamed *Sendan* and *Kandan*.

I Class

Displacement:	750–790 tons
Length:	246ft
Beam:	26.75ft
Draught:	8.5ft
Armament:	Two 4in guns, two 12pdr guns, one 3pdr AA gun, two 21in torpedoes
Machinery:	16,500–20,000hp
Speed:	30–32kt

These were similar, in armament and size, apart from having the addition of a 3-pounder anti-aircraft gun. This significant development was followed in most subsequent classes. However, they were faster and more powerful than the H Class, having 16,500–20,000hp. All had two funnels.

Archer and *Attack* used superheated steam on an experimental basis and *Badger* and *Beaver* had geared turbines. *Ariel* struck a mine while itself laying mines in the North Sea, and *Attack* and *Phoenix* were torpedoed by U-boats in the Mediterranean and Adriatic respectively.

Defender was an I Class destroyer launched in 1911. The structure aft of the second funnel is a searchlight.

K Class

Displacement:	934–984 tons
Length:	267.5ft
Beam:	27ft
Draught:	9.5ft
Armament:	Three 4in guns, one 2pdr gun, two 21in torpedoes
Machinery:	22,500–25,000hp
Speed:	31kt

These ships had three funnels and three 4in guns, one in the "A" position and one either side of the second torpedo tube, or in some cases one before and one aft of the tube. These vessels continued the trend towards more speed and power, being rated at 22,500–25,000hp.

Four of these ships were lost at the Battle of Jutland in 1916 – *Ardent*, *Fortune*, *Shark* and *Sparrowhawk*. *Contest* was sunk by a U-boat, *Lynx* was mined, and *Paragon* was sunk by a German destroyer in the Dover Strait in March 1917.

L Class

Displacement:	965–1,003 tons
Length:	296ft
Beam:	29.75ft
Draught:	9.5ft
Armament:	Three 4in guns, one 2pdr gun, four 21in torpedoes
Machinery:	22,500–24,500hp
Speed:	29kt

These were slightly slower and less powerful than their predecessors. Some had two and some three funnels. *Laforey* and *Leonidas* had geared turbines and *Legion* was configured as a minelayer. The three 4in guns were positioned

Lance being launched at the Thorneycroft yard in 1914. Britain built 294 destroyers during World War I, under the emergency warship programme. The L Class ships were heavily armed, with three 4in guns, but were too slow to work with the battlefleet.

one in the "A" position, one in the "Y" position and one on a "bandstand" between the funnels. They had turbines developing 22,500–24,500hp.

Louis was wrecked in Suvla Bay, Gallipoli, in 1915, *Laforey* mined in the English Channel and *Lassoo* torpedoed by a U-boat.

M Class

Displacement:	879–1,070 tons
Length:	271–274ft
Beam:	27.5ft
Draught:	10.5ft
Armament:	Three 4in guns, one 2pdr gun, four 21in torpedoes
Machinery:	25,000–27,000hp
Speed:	34–36kt

These were derived from the L Class but were slightly faster and more powerful. They were the most numerous class built, with variants by Thorneycroft, Yarrow and Hawthorn. They were the classic fleet destroyers. Standard M Class ships had three funnels, while Hawthorn-built ships had four and Yarrow-built ships two. M class were excellent, powerful ships rated at 25,000–27,000hp that played a major part in wartime fighting.

Some early M Class ships had separate cruising turbines to improve economy. They were considered easy to build and outfit and many of them were able to achieve much higher speeds than the official maximum of 34kt. Some vessels were fitted out to carry kite balloons. Their 4in guns were positioned as on L Class ships.

Nestor and *Nomad* were lost at Jutland and *Nessus* and *Marmion* in collisions. *Narborough* and *Opal* were both lost in a savage storm off Orkney

ABOVE TOP
Moresby was one of the 110 M Class destroyers built between 1914 and 1916. With three 4in guns, 21in torpedoes and a speed of 34kt, these were excellent ships; they formed the backbone of the Grand Fleet's destroyer force. Note the "bandstand" beneath the ensign, on which a 4in gun was mounted.

ABOVE
An M Class destroyer going at full speed to take up station ahead of the battlefleet. In the background is one of the British dreadnoughts, possibly *Iron Duke*.

in January 1918. *North Star* was sunk by gunfire during the Zeebrugge raid, *Partridge* was sunk by the gunfire of four German destroyers while escorting a convoy, *Mary Rose* was sunk by German cruisers also while on convoy duties, and *Pheasant* was mined off Orkney. *Surprise* and *Ulleswater*, both Yarrow-built variants of the M Class ships, were lost late in the war, to mines and a U-boat respectively.

R Class

Displacement:	1,040 tons
Length:	276ft
Beam:	26.75ft
Draught:	10.5ft
Armament:	Three 4in guns, one 2pdr gun, four 21in torpedoes
Machinery:	27,000hp
Speed:	36kt

The adoption of geared turbines made these relatively faster and more economical ships, and some of them remained in service long after the war. In most other aspects they were very similar to the M Class vessels, except that the after 4in gun was mounted on a bandstand, as well as the midships gun. *Tarpon* and *Telemachus* were minelayers. Some Thorneycroft-built R Class destroyers differed from the standard in having three funnels and slightly more

Vimiera was one of the powerful V Class destroyers built in 1918. They were derived from the ex-Turkish ships but were much better armed, with four 4in guns director-controlled from above the bridge and mounted in the "A", "B", "X" and "Y" positions, giving an improved arc of fire. Note the anti-aircraft gun position aft of the second funnel. Most ships of this class had a rangefinder mounted above the bridge structure. They were extensively used in World War II and played an important role in the Battle of the Atlantic. *Vimiera* was mined in 1942.

power (29,000hp). They were particularly fast; *Teaser* is reported to have exceeded 40kt in trials. *Radiant* was transferred to the Royal Siamese Navy, being renamed *Phra Ruang*.

Recruit was mined, *Tornado* and *Torrent* were both sunk by mines off the Maas lightship in December 1917, and *Simoon* was sunk by gunfire from German destroyers.

S, V and W Classes

Displacement:	1,075 tons
Length:	276ft
Beam:	26.75ft
Draught:	10.5ft
Armament:	S Class: Three 4in guns, one 2pdr gun, four 21in torpedoes, 30 depth charges
	V & W Class: Four 4in guns
Machinery:	27,000hp
Speed:	36kt

Typical specifications, some major variations existed within and between these classes.

These fine ships were completed too late to see much action in World War I, but many of them were sunk by the Japanese in World War II. However, many of the W Class also proved very effective convoy escorts in the Battle of the Atlantic and were not scrapped until well after 1945. In addition to the normal armament they carried depth charges and in some cases two 14in torpedoes on either beam for use in night actions. Some were later fitted with aircraft catapults and one, *Shakari*, was adapted to control remotely operated battleships – an idea tested during the interwar years. V and W class ships had four 4in guns in the "A", "B", "X" and "Y" positions. These were director-controlled from a position aft of the bridge.

Two Thorneycroft-designed ships, *Wishart* and *Witch*, were ordered in 1917, following the same general specification as the W Class but with slightly different dimensions, being beamier and of slightly larger displacement. Their engines were also more powerful, rated at 30,000hp against 27,000hp. However, production of these was delayed and they were not launched until the 1920s.

Marksman was launched in 1916. It was a flotilla leader following the general design and layout of the ex-Chilean destroyers commandeered by the Admiralty. These were much bigger than the ex-Turkish ships (1,600 tons against 1,100 tons). They mounted four 4in guns and two anti-aircraft guns, and there were two double 21in torpedo tubes.

Flotilla leaders

Flotilla leaders were urgently required to act as lead ships for destroyer flotillas. At the outbreak of war *Swift* was the only purpose-built leader with accommodation for a senior officer and his staff. Fortunately, however, some suitable large destroyers were on the stocks designated for Turkey, Greece and Chile, and these were commandeered for the Royal Navy. They were given the class designations Talisman (Turkish and Greek) and Botha (Chilean).

	Ex-Turkish (Talisman)	Ex-Chile (Botha)
Builder:	Hawthorn Leslie	White
Displacement:	1,098 tons	1,800 tons
Length:	309ft	331ft
Beam:	28ft	32ft
Draught:	9ft 6in	11ft
Armament:	Five 4in guns, four 21in tubes	Two 4.7in and two 4in guns, four 21in tubes
Machinery:	25,000hp	30,000hp
Speed:	32kt	32kt
Fuel:	238 tons oil	403 tons coal, 83 tons oil

Note: The ex-Greek ships differed in some minor details from the ex-Turkish ones.

MARKSMAN AND W CLASS

Nimrod (1)

The Marksman Class flotilla leader *Nimrod*, built by Denny in 1915, has four 4in guns, four 21in torpedo tubes and two two-pounder anti-aircraft guns. Note the extensive space aft for senior officers' quarters.

Wild Swan (2)

This W Class destroyer was completed too late for World War I, but many of its fellows did take part from early 1918 onward. Note the very heavy gun armament (four 4.7in director-controlled guns). These ships also had geared turbines, making the propulsion system much more efficient. W Class destroyers continued to be built in the interwar period and played a major role in World War II. *Wild Swan* was sunk by air attack in 1942. Although very vulnerable to aircraft these proved excellent convoy escorts and accounted for numerous U-boats in World War II.

A comparison between *Wild Swan* (1919) and *Velox* (1902) highlights how far destroyers had evolved in the space of fewer than 20 years.

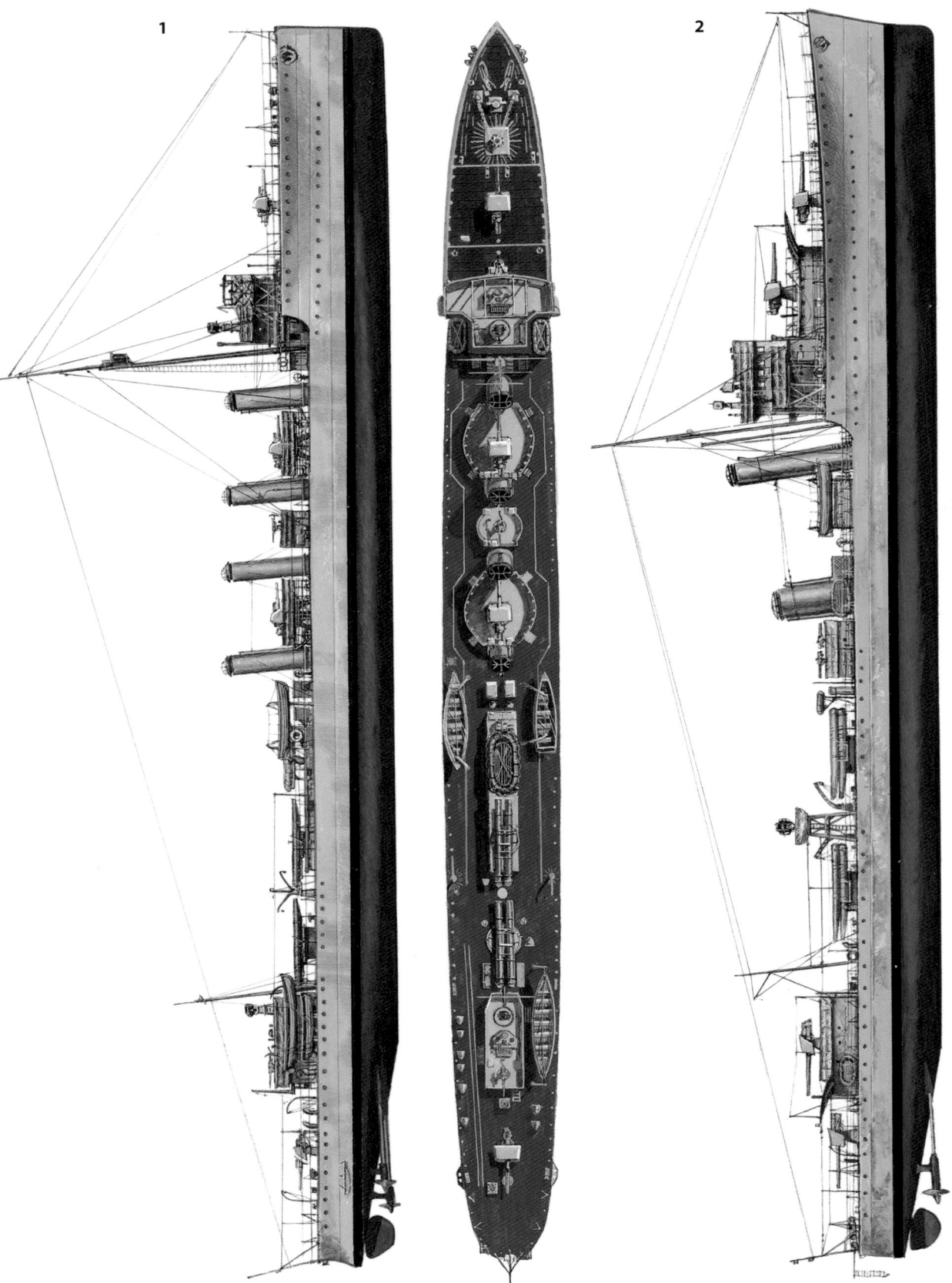

Talisman was an ex-Turkish flotilla leader. These proved to be excellent ships – fast enough to lead a flotilla of M Class destroyers, and heavily armed with five 4in guns and two double 21in torpedo tubes. Note the two 4in guns side by side on the foredeck.

These proved excellent ships, but there were only four of each class and the rapidly increasing destroyer fleet required many more leaders. The first of these were of the Marksman Class, which were quite similar to the Chilean specification apart from their armament and fuel. One ship of the class, *Abdiel*, was fitted out as a fast minelayer.

Tipperary (Botha Class) was sunk by gunfire at Jutland. *Medusa* (ex-Greek) was lost in a collision off the German coast.

The Marksman Class was followed by the Anzac Class and then by what was known as the Admiralty Large Design (also referred to as the Scott Class); some of these were only completed just after the war.

Two further Thorneycroft-built ships, constituting what is known as the Shakespeare Class (*Shakespeare* and *Spencer*), were built generally to the Admiralty Large Design and completed in 1917. *Scott* (Admiralty Large) was sunk by a U-boat in August 1918.

	Marksman	Anzac	Admiralty Large
Displacement:	1,600 tons	1,670 tons	1,800 tons
Length:	321ft	325ft	322ft
Beam:	31ft 9in	31ft 9in	31ft 9in
Draught:	11ft	10ft 6in	12ft 6in
Armament:	Four 4in guns, four 21in tubes	Four 4in guns, four 21in tubes	Five 4.7in guns, six 21in tubes
Machinery:	36,000hp	36,000hp	40,000hp geared
Speed:	34kt	34kt	36.5kt
Fuel:	510 tons oil	415 tons oil	500 tons oil

GUN ARMAMENT

When these craft first came into service in the 1890s, the Royal Navy was still operating warships with muzzle loading main armament. These had an unconscionably low rate of fire, and even some of the large breechloaders took seven minutes to reload. However, the revolutionary "quick-firers" fitted to TBDs were manually loaded and fitted with an easily operated breech mechanism. They were aimed by the gunlayer using a shoulder rest and optical gunsight, and usually protected by a simple shield (it seems that in practice, this was not always fitted). There was always a compromise to be made between designs using either a large number of six-pounders or a smaller number of 12-pounders. Proponents of the smaller guns pointed out the higher chance of gaining hits with a deluge of fire from many small weapons and the difficulty of aiming single shots accurately on a small, lively, craft in a seaway. As the intended quarry would be a lightly built torpedo-boat, six-pounder hits would be quite adequate. However, the big-gun party gradually prevailed due to the ever-wider range of tasks envisaged for destroyers, many requiring longer range and greater hitting power. It was also argued that having many smaller guns demanded a larger crew. Thus, as destroyers evolved the standard armament became heavier and heavier, culminating in the excellent 4.7in weapons mounted on the later classes of flotilla leader.

These were director-controlled guns – centrally aimed by a gunnery officer situated high up over the bridge structure. The guns were mounted behind armoured shields and power-rotated. Local control could be assumed if necessary. Gun specifications were as shown in the table below.

A 3.3in anti-aircraft gun. The later stages of the war saw some spirited engagements with aircraft.

Calibre	Muzzle velocity	Weight	Rounds/min	Penetration*	Use
2.24in	1,740ft/sec	6lb	20	n/a	Early TBDs
3.0in	2,500ft/sec	12lb	20	2.4in	Early TBDs
4.0in	2,300ft/sec	25 or 31lb	15	3.3in	F Class *et seq.*
4.7in	3,000ft/sec	55 or 65lb	15	4.5in	Flotilla leaders
6.0in	2,400ft/sec	100lb	12	8.2in	*Swift* only

* This was the calculated thickness of Krupp steel which could be perforated at 3,000yd. It was a theoretical figure only, to provide a standard of comparison. In practice penetration was nowhere near this figure.

Note: 80–100 rounds per gun were normally carried.

As time went on a great variety of other weapons were fitted, including Vickers heavy machine-guns, anti-aircraft guns of various types, and light multi-barrelled pom-poms.

THE DESTROYER FLEETS IN 1914 AND 1918

The composition of the British destroyer fleet at the outbreak of the war is set out in the table below.

A, B, C and D classes	100 (many converted to other duties or in reserve)
River Class	35
Tribal Class	12
Swift	1
G Class	16
H Class	20
I Class	23
K Class	20
L Class	13
Total	**240**

Germany's destroyer fleet at the time comprised some 130 vessels. Britain built 294 destroyers during the war, as detailed in the table below.

L Class	9
M Class	110
Ex-Turkish	4
Ex-Greek	4
Ex-Chilean	4
Marksman	7
Anzac	6
R Class	55
S Class	34
V and W Class	53
Admiralty Large	8 (including Shakespeare Class)
Total	**294**

 AN M CLASS DESTROYER FIRING A 21IN TORPEDO AT JUTLAND

In daylight it was very difficult for destroyers to get close enough to an enemy ship to have much chance of scoring a hit, but in the dark or poor daytime visibility they were sometimes able to approach undetected. A 21in torpedo hit would probably not be terminal for a dreadnought-type German capital ship fitted with anti-torpedo bulkheads, but it would probably slow it down. Such a torpedo would be likely to sink a light cruiser or a destroyer, however.

Only 102 German destroyers were built during the war, because priority was given to other types of weapon and later to submarines, and because of the critical shortage of strategic materials. This was just as well for Britain as some of the later German destroyers were extremely formidable ships; examples are given in the table below.

Type	Tonnage	Guns	Torpedo tubes	Speed
S13–S24	568	Two 4.1in	Four 19.7in	35kt
S53–S66	919	Three 4.1in	Six 19.7in	35kt
V67–V84	934	Three 4.1in	Six 19.7in	36kt
G85–G95	960	Three 4.1in	Six 19.7in	34kt
G101–G104	1120	Four 4.1in	Four 19.7in	33kt
B97–98 and B109–112	1374	Four 4.1in	Four 19.7in	37kt

Seventy British and 67 German destroyers were lost during the war. Causes are set out in the table below.

	British	German
Mined	22	33
Collision	14	5
Surface action	13	14
Sunk by submarine	11*	3
Wrecked	8	3
Rammed	2	2
Scuttled to avoid capture	0	7

* Ten British vessels were sunk by German and one by Austro-Hungarian submarines.

During the war British destroyers sank 13 U-boats, one battleship (*Pommern*) and a host of smaller craft including at least ten German destroyers.

The main function of the British destroyer force early in the war was to deny the enemy easy access to the Channel and to retain overall command of the North Sea. They constantly battled the gales, fogs and manmade hazards such as minefields. They harassed enemy minelayers, forced U-boats to travel submerged, intercepted neutral ships carrying supplies to Germany, covered shore bombardments by heavily gunned warships and escorted friendly vessels of all descriptions. They were used extensively for laying offensive mines close to the German coast. Destroyers also had the vital role of providing a protective screen for the main battlefleet – acting as scouts and warding off submarines and torpedo-boats. They played a major role in actions between battlefleets by threatening major warships with their torpedoes.

Swift's formidable 6in gun.

From 1917 onwards the German navy concentrated on trying to cut Britain off from its empire and from the US by using submarines on an unrestricted basis. From this point British (and American) destroyers played the leading role in protecting the convoys which were to save the day, albeit narrowly, for the Entente powers. Some illustrations of how the different roles were performed are provided in a subsequent chapter.

Both sides exaggerated the potential of torpedoes fired by surface vessels before and during the war, as is demonstrated by the statistics relating to the Battle of Jutland given below. Overreliance on the potential of torpedoes and the destroyers which launched them was a particular error on the German side. British destroyers were better suited to acting in independent roles and as "maids-of-all-work", with more emphasis placed on gun armament and independent action than was the case with their opponents.

Refuelling at sea from a battleship. Destroyers only carried fuel for about 1,500 miles at cruising speed and the range was much less than this if they were travelling fast. Easy refuelling at sea was one advantage over coal burners.

DESTROYERS IN COMBAT 1914–1918

Action off Texel (17 October 1914)

This action early in the war was relatively minor in scale, but had disproportionate consequences for the outcome of the struggle. Four British L Class destroyers – *Legion*, *Loyal*, *Lance* and *Lennox* – accompanied by the light cruiser *Undaunted* (under Capt Cecil Fox) were sweeping northwards when they saw the smoke of four unidentified small ships coming towards them in line abreast. This was in fact the German 7th Half-Flotilla under Cdr August Thiele, comprising the destroyers *S115*, *S117*, *S118*, and *S119* – all 29kt ships built around 1903. The German ships were steaming south with the intention of laying mines in the path of British ships bombarding the Belgian coast.

The contest was an unequal one. British destroyers were designed with just such an encounter in mind and mounted 4in guns, while the German philosophy was to use destroyers as an adjunct to the battle fleet rather than as independent fighting vessels, so German destroyers mounted only 3.3in guns. The British also had the support of the 6in guns of *Undaunted*. Fox initially believed that the destroyers he had met were the advance screen of a stronger force, of battlecruisers perhaps. Nevertheless, he made up his mind to finish his

The light cruiser *Undaunted*. Its 6in main armament made for an easy victory in the action off Texel against older German destroyers.

opponents off as quickly as possible, then retire. Each British destroyer was allocated one opponent to chase, with *Undaunted* in support in case of trouble. The Germans, for their part, realised that they could not outrun the enemy and that their best hope was to close to within torpedo range.

A spirited engagement took place, with ships manoeuvring at high speed and continually altering course, which made accurate gunfire difficult. The British expended almost 100 six-inch and 900 four-inch shells, making up for lack of accuracy with rate of fire.

S118 was rapidly put out of action by gunfire from *Undaunted* and from two of the British destroyers at a range of 2,500yd. *S117* and *S119* then boldly approached *Undaunted*, seeking to torpedo it, but the cruiser wisely turned away; at the same moment *Legion* appeared on the scene, guns blazing. *S117* fired three torpedoes at *Legion*, but one passed ahead, another astern and a third clean underneath it. *Legion's* guns soon damaged the German's steering gear and *S117* was rapidly reduced to a wreck.

Loyal then engaged *S119*, opening fire at 3,500yd but without effect. The British ship's aft gun was put out of action; nevertheless, it closed range and soon gained the upper hand. *S119's* final act was to fire a torpedo at *Lance*, which had joined the fight. However, although the torpedo hit *Lance* amidships it did not explode and caused minimal damage.

The final phase of the action was between *Lennox* and *S115*, which refused to surrender even though it was reduced to a complete wreck. *S115* continued to fire its Maxim machine guns at *Lennox*, although this could do no serious damage. Eventually *S115* sank, leaving only a single survivor. This incident offered an early and impressive demonstration of the fine fighting spirit of the German navy.

Having destroyed his opponents and sighted no supporting enemy force, Capt Fox ordered *Loyal* back to Harwich with the prisoners and the three British casualties – *Loyal's* first lieutenant and members of the crew of the aft gun which had been hit by two four-pounder shells, probably from *S119*. Fox's other vessels were undamaged and he continued his sweep to the north.

 BRITISH DESTROYERS GOING INTO ACTION AT JUTLAND
Building up to 35kt, the destroyers pulled past Beatty's battlecruisers, cut across their bows and attacked the enemy line, encountering a force of German destroyers engaged on a similar mission. Waterspouts from the secondary armament of the rival battlecruisers and from the light cruisers erupted all around them, adding to the general mayhem. In the general melee which followed destroyers on both sides were fatally damaged. It proved impossible for destroyers to approach capital ships closely enough to achieve many torpedo hits, the only successful one being by *Petard* on *Seydlitz*.

The vital significance of this engagement emerged on 30 November. By chance, a British trawler netted the codebooks which had been jettisoned by *S119*. Unusually, *S119* had been carrying the books for the highest-level German code, "VB" code, used for interservice and diplomatic communications. Such material was not normally risked aboard warships; perhaps on this occasion *S119* had needed them to communicate with army units advancing through Belgium. The codebooks found their way to British Naval Intelligence, enabling the British to read the highest-level enemy communications, including the fateful Zimmermann telegram which brought the US into the war on the Entente nations' side. No wonder the catch made on 30 November was known as "the miraculous draught of fishes".

The action off Texel vindicated the British practice of building destroyers with powerful gun armament, suitable for establishing and maintaining command of the North Sea. In this type of fast-moving action torpedoes proved less effective than German planners had hoped.

THE BATTLE OF JUTLAND (31 MAY 1916)

Jutland was the only major clash between rival battlefleets in the war. German commanders had high hopes for their modern seagoing destroyer force, the ships of which were at least equal in speed and torpedo armament to the best in the Royal Navy. The German force included the latest types of destroyer mounting 4.1in guns, and six 19.7in torpedo tubes, which should have been more than a match for the British M Class ships. In fact, there were many destroyer actions at Jutland; the incidents described below will provide some examples of the performance of British forces.

Eighty-five British destroyers were deployed at Jutland, against 72 German. Eight British were lost (including one flotilla leader) to five German. German commanders commented that the British destroyer crews were badly trained for night action and generally approached their targets too closely before releasing torpedoes, suffering excessive damage as a result. In fact the British destroyers inflicted far more damage than the German, and at Jutland German destroyers did not display the daring and aggression typical of them in other encounters.

The run to the south

The first phase of the battle was the clash – disastrous from the British point of view – between Beatty's six battlecruisers and Hipper's five. During the action the British *Indefatigable* and *Queen Mary* were sunk. In the thick of the action Beatty ordered a torpedo attack by the 9th, 10th and 13th flotillas, consisting of 12 ships – mostly M Class vessels – led by the light cruiser *Champion*.

Abdiel was a Marksman Class destroyer adapted as a fast minelayer. The strange-looking structure on the after deck is screening for 60–70 mines.

Immediately the order was given the smaller ships built up to 35kt and cut across the bows of the British flagship, *Lion*, in line astern, bow waves creaming and sterns buried deep in the water. Officers on the battlecruisers remarked on what a fine sight they made. The destroyer crews were determined to show what they could do in action. They

Mines were by far the most effective weapons in World War I. Here the super-dreadnought *Audacious* is sinking after striking a single mine laid by the German converted liner *Berlin*. Two destroyers stand by.

were soon between the two fleets of battlecruisers, manoeuvring to get close enough to the Germans to deliver an effective torpedo attack. The ideal position would be just ahead of the enemy on his starboard bow.

However, Hipper saw what was happening and countered by sending 15 of his own destroyers, led by the light cruiser *Regensburg*, to intercept the attackers. The German force consisted of a mix of classes, including several of the formidable new S53–S66 Class. There were thus some 30 small ships charging towards each other at a closing speed of some 70kt, while the heavy shells of the great battlecruisers whizzed overhead and waterspouts from their secondary armament erupted all round the destroyers. A fierce firefight soon broke out between the rival destroyer forces, which blazed away at each other at point blank range. The German *V29* was hit by a torpedo from *Petard* and *V27* by gunfire, but the guns of *Regensburg* proved devastatingly effective, disabling the British destroyer *Nomad*. Six of the Germans got close enough to the British battlecruisers to launch ten torpedoes, but all missed and the initial German attack petered out. About 15 minutes later another group of German destroyers got a better opportunity as the British battlecruisers passed the four fast battleships of Admiral Evan Thomas's 5BS, which had come to their aid. These big ships passing each other presented a very large target. However, although seven more torpedoes were fired, all missed.

On the British side, *Nestor* and *Nicator* got within 6,000yd of the German battle line and fired torpedoes, but these also failed to hit their target. The British ships then turned away, regrouped, and fired again from a closer range at *Lützow* and *Derfflinger*, but again without success. The little ships then blazed away at their adversaries with their 4in guns, scoring several hits but doing little damage. *Nestor* suffered a hit from *Regensburg's* guns and was brought to a stop.

By this time Beatty had ordered the destroyers to break off their action, but like excited terriers they were deaf to his commands. *Petard* and *Turbulent* made two torpedo attacks, the second one on *Seydlitz*. This time one of the torpedoes struck home. German capital ships of the time had an excellent arrangement of anti-torpedo bulkheads and were extremely well constructed. However, although *Seydlitz* was able to resume its place in the line after a few minutes, the damage was considerable: one 5.9in gun was dismounted, the outer hull was ruptured, and severe leaks started which eventually put much of the ship's electrical gear out of action. This damage, combined with subsequent shell hits, almost caused *Seydlitz* to sink. It was eventually towed into Wilhelmshaven and repairs were completed by 16 September.

Returning to station, *Petard* offered to tow the disabled *Nestor* but the offer was refused. Just at that moment there appeared over the horizon the terrifying sight of the German battlefleet, which the British commanders had been informed was in harbour. At least one destroyer, *Moorsom*, immediately switched its attention from the enemy battlecruisers to the main battlefleet and charged towards it, releasing torpedoes at 8,500yd. Yet again, these missed, and the destroyer was hit by a 5.9in shell which brought down the mast, leaving it trailing over the side. The debris was cut away and *Moorsom* turned round and repeated its assault on the battleships, but once again missing its target. It had a hot time returning to the British line under a deluge of fire. Destroyer captains in these circumstances had two choices of tactic. One was to steer for the last shell burst on the theory that the next one would not fall in the same place. The other was to watch the guns of the assailant and as soon as they flashed make a violent turn so that the ship was never on the expected spot when the shells reached it. Using this tactic *Moorsom* was able to regain the safety of the British line.

This action demonstrated the weaknesses of destroyers in a fleet action in daylight. Hitting a fast-moving ship with a torpedo under battle conditions was extremely difficult, and retaining any formation or order in the heat of battle was almost impossible. The experience also showed how well the German battlecruisers were constructed, since a 21in torpedo strike on a British ship would have had much more serious consequences. British ships were less heavily armoured and more lightly built than German ships, so were far more liable to serious damage from a mine or torpedo strike. For example, a single German mine had sunk the new superdreadnought *Audacious* in 1914.

Night action

The final phase of the battle was the escape by the German High Seas Fleet, achieved by cutting through the rear of the British Grand Fleet during the night and the early morning of 1 June. This led to a number of confused actions mostly involving destroyers and light cruisers.

At about 0200hr, when dawn was just beginning to break, 14 destroyers of the British 12th Flotilla found themselves close to the German 5th Division, which at that point consisted of 11 battleships supported by destroyers and light cruisers. In the semidarkness it was extremely difficult to keep in contact with the enemy and to retain any sort of formation while avoiding collisions between friendly ships, but eventually ten destroyers, mostly M Class but led by *Faulkner*, an ex-Chilean flotilla leader, managed to mount an attack. As soon as the enemy vessels identified their attackers they opened fire with their 5.9in secondary armament and turned away from their assailants. Torpedoes were launched at ranges of 3,000–1,700yd; one of them, fired by *Onslaught*, hit the old battleship *Pommern*, which went down with its crew of 850 men. There was a series of violent and sporadic engagements as ships loomed out of the morning mist and gloom, but the destroyers managed to get away with only one serious hit from an enemy shell, on *Onslaught's* bridge, which killed the captain and first lieutenant. As the destroyers drew off they laid a smokescreen for protection. The noise and commotion attracted the attention of other small ships on both sides and they blazed away at each other, but without much effect. By this time many of the destroyers on both sides had expended all their torpedoes. All of the 12th Flotilla arrived home safely, although the heavily damaged *Onslaught* had lost all its charts and navigational gear, which caused its surviving officers some challenging problems.

This action, which might easily have had more serious consequences for the Germans, showed how darkness enabled destroyers to operate at reasonably close ranges with acceptable risk of damage, and use their torpedoes effectively.

However, British techniques for fighting and communication in darkness left much to be desired and an opportunity was missed.

Minelaying

Mines were by far the deadliest weapons during the 1914–18 naval war, and all sides converted some destroyers (as well as other types of craft) into minelayers. During the Battle of Jutland the British made use of the great speed of a destroyer thus converted to attempt to block off one of the German channels of escape.

At 9.30pm on 31 May the Marksman Class flotilla leader *Abdiel* was ordered to lay a cargo of mines off Horns Reef, an area of shallows off the Danish coast. This was not the first time the destroyer had operated in the area, as it had laid mines there in early May. *Abdiel* had spent the early stages of the Battle of Jutland as part of the destroyer force flanking the Grand Fleet and was positioned close to the flagship *Iron Duke* when it received the order. *Abdiel* immediately worked up to 32kt and headed for the reef. On this type of mission speed and secrecy were of paramount importance. *Abdiel* was able to make its way past a number of hostile formations without being noticed, as it was an efficient oil burner and produced almost no smoke. Accurate navigation must have been difficult in the nighttime with haze obscuring the stars, but the destroyer reached its position at 1am and laid 90 mines in the approaches to the deepwater channel. It then steamed back to the Royal Navy base at Rosyth, Scotland, and reloaded with mines.

These missions had not been in vain. The German battleship *Ostfriesland* struck one of the mines, probably one laid during the earlier mission, and was severely damaged, although once again the superb defensive armour of the German ships enabled the battleship to keep going.

Lessons from Jutland

Before 1914 many naval analysts expected destroyers to play a pivotal role in any fleet encounter; the Germans in particular were convinced this would be the case. The major miscalculation was overestimation of the effectiveness of torpedo attacks by small vessels. Peacetime exercises had suggested that 30 per cent of torpedoes fired in action would hit their targets. In practice, in the heat of battle targeting was far less accurate. The British fired 96 torpedoes at Jutland and scored six hits, while the Germans fired 105 and scored two or possibly three hits. Thus the proportion of hits was less than 5 per cent overall. Five of the successful British torpedo launches were from destroyers

An M Class destroyer launching a kite balloon for observation.

41

(*Petard* one, *Onslaught* one, *Ambuscade* or *Contest* one, *Onslow* one, and either *Petard* or *Turbulent* one). One or possibly two German destroyers hit their mark (*S54* one, and possibly *V71* one). There is a strong possibility that the depth control and firing mechanisms used on German torpedoes at the time were unreliable, which may account for their poor performance.

The actual damage done by torpedoes varied. British torpedo strikes sank the pre-dreadnought battleship *Pommern*, the light cruisers *Frauenlob* and *Rostock*, and the destroyer *V29*. They also caused severe damage to the battlecruiser *Seydlitz* and the light cruiser *Wiesbaden*. Apart from *Frauenlob*, which was sunk by the British light cruiser *Southampton*, all these torpedoes were fired by destroyers. On the other side, the battleship *Marlborough* was damaged by a torpedo, but not fatally, and the destroyer *Shark* was sunk by one. The conclusion drawn from this is that while torpedo-firing destroyers could indeed destroy small or obsolete warships, they were unlikely to prove fatal when used against well-designed modern capital ships.

However, the fear of destroyer action did have a pronounced effect on how the battlefleets were handled. For example, just before nightfall an attack on the Grand Fleet by massed German destroyers forced the British fleet to turn away, saving the battered German battleships and battlecruisers from being overwhelmed by the British, who were in an ideal position to "cross their T". Smoke floats dropped by the German destroyers as they turned made it impossible for British gunfire to be effective. None of the volley of torpedoes fired by the Germans in this manoeuvre found their mark, but their action nevertheless saved the day.

It was proving extremely difficult to aim a torpedo accurately in action from the deck of a fast small ship. Even if the aim was perfect, the torpedo's speed of about 40kt meant it would take several minutes to reach its objective, which might itself be steaming at anything between 22kt and 35kt and was almost certainly not steering a steady course. Torpedoes fired at long range could also be pushed off course by the propeller wash of a big ship which had turned away from its assailant. This may account for the ineffectiveness of the German massed assault. It seems surprising in retrospect not that so few hits were obtained, but rather that anyone expected any better result.

The wheelhouse of *Swift*.

THE DOVER PATROL

It was vital for the Entente powers to keep the English Channel safe for the transport of troops and supplies from England to France. It was also important to make it too dangerous for U-boats to pass down the Channel to their hunting grounds in the Western Approaches. To achieve this a complicated system of nets, mines and obstructions was placed across the eastern end of the channel, and this was constantly patrolled by armed trawlers and drifters. Instant reinforcement could be summoned from the battleships, cruisers and destroyers available to the admiral commanding Dover. Due to the narrowness of the Dover Strait and shallows such as the Varne bank in the middle of it, most of the patrol work fell to destroyers.

When the Germans reverted to unrestricted submarine warfare after Jutland, it became especially important for their U-boats to pass safely down the Channel. To assist them in this 40 destroyers and torpedo-boats were based at Bruges and Zeebrugge in Belgium with the task of harassing the defenders of the barrage, and if possible gaining the upper hand over the Dover force. A number of vigorous encounters occurred in which German raiders were able to do a considerable amount of damage, including sinking the destroyers *Flirt* and *Simoon* and a large number of drifters.

Officers of *Swift* after the action in the Dover Strait.

On the night of 20 April 1917 the large and powerful, flotilla leader *Swift*, which had recently been fitted with a 6in gun, and *Broke*, one of the ex-Chilean ships, were in Calais harbour expecting to escort the F Class destroyer *Amazon* carrying important dignitaries across the Channel. Suddenly a burst of gunfire was heard from seaward. A force of 12 German destroyers was making a nighttime raid on the barrage and its defenders. The German destroyers included some 35kt, 960-ton G85–G95 class vessels, similar in size to the British R Class. However, their 4.1in guns were no match for *Swift's* 6in weapon. The German ships had a critical disadvantage when operating at night: being coal burners, their funnels emitted sparks and flames when they were steaming fast, which made them easy to detect in the darkness.

Swift (under Commander A. M. Peck) and *Broke* (Commander Edward Evans) soon made out the attackers and Peck tried to ram the nearest, *G42*, but missed. However, *Broke* hit *G42* full amidships, almost cutting it in half. The German crew stormed onto *Broke's* foredeck and a savage hand-to-hand fight ensued; however, a petty officer with a light machine-gun soon had the boarders subdued and they were taken below as prisoners. An officer was surprised a little while later to find them being served a hearty meal of bacon and eggs by their captors. *Swift* in the meantime had swung round and torpedoed *G85*, which sank, then completed the destruction of *G42*. The other Germans made their escape in the darkness, and *Swift* towed the damaged *Broke* safely home, having picked up most of the German survivors.

Amazingly this was the second time *Broke* had been damaged by collision. At Jutland, heavily damaged by gunfire, it had collided with the British destroyer *Sparrowhawk*. On that occasion the vessel had just been able to limp home. This action brought some satisfaction to the Dover force, which generally had a tough time patrolling the barrage, and it made the Germans more circumspect about attacking the force with surface ships. However, U-boats did still manage to creep down Channel and their mines and torpedoes were a constant menace to the defenders.

ESCORT DUTY

The Entente powers came extremely close to defeat during the war when unrestricted submarine warfare almost succeeded in cutting Britain's supply lines. While cross-Channel traffic and some sailings to Scandinavia were escorted by armed trawlers or destroyers, long-distance freighters were unprotected and made easy prey for the torpedoes, or more often the deck guns, of U-boats. In the first three months of 1917 two million tons of shipping fell victim to the U-boat campaign. The Admiralty had bitterly resisted the introduction of convoys, arguing among other things, that there were too few destroyers to protect both convoys and the Grand Fleet.

Destroyers had not been designed primarily as anti-submarine vessels, but by 1917 many of them had been equipped with depth charges and hydrophones which in good conditions could detect the movement of a submerged U-boat two miles away. Clearly these ships could become effective protectors of merchantmen on the especially dangerous segments of their journeys in the Western Approaches and coastal waters. Political pressure on the Admiralty forced it to change its tune, and in May 1917 the first experiments with large deep-sea convoys began. The merchantmen were escorted by armed trawlers or cruisers for most of their voyage, then destroyers took over for the critical part of the journey, in the U-boat hunting grounds of the Western Approaches. U-boats were slow underwater so it was impossible for them to manoeuvre into a position to attack a convoy without surfacing, and they could not risk doing this when destroyers were present. There was also obviously no chance of using their gun armament in the face of the far more effective guns mounted by destroyers. For these reasons, the convoy system was a resounding success. Fortunately, its introduction coincided with the arrival of a large number of large, long-range American destroyers which, from their base in Cork Harbour, Ireland, proved extremely effective convoy escorts. Gradually, U-boat losses increased while those of merchant shipping declined. The Grand Fleet complained that it could only find some 30 destroyers to escort it to sea whereas it needed 100, but continued American arrivals and the energetic British building programme enabled continuous development of the convoy system.

However, there were some nasty surprises in store for the British. In 1914 German yards had started work on components for two battlecruisers ordered by the Imperial Russian Navy. The advent of war meant components for these became available to the Kaiser's navy, and the Vulcan yard at Stettin incorporated them into two very fast minelaying cruisers, armed with four 5.9in guns and capable of more than 28kt. They were named *Brummer* and *Bremse*. As the U-boats were having a hard time by autumn 1917, the Germans decided to use these formidable ships to make a surprise raid on shipping on the Scandinavian route.

The Admiralty was able to read almost all German signals traffic and was aware that the two cruisers were putting to sea, but imagined that they would be deployed, as usual, as minelayers. No one at the Admiralty thought to tell Beatty, in command at Scapa Flow, that these formidable ships had set out, and he authorised the departure of a convoy consisting of two British, one Belgian and nine neutral merchantmen. This was lightly escorted by two

G **THE BATTLE OF HELIGOLAND BIGHT**

In the confused action known as the Battle of Heligoland Bight, British I and L Class destroyers and light cruisers went into action against a strong force of German ships. The situation looked serious until Beatty's battlecruiser force arrived on the scene, saving the day for the British. The Germans lost three light cruisers and a destroyer. All the British ships got home. This illustration shows a division of I Class destroyers led by *Acheron* forming up to make a torpedo attack on a German light cruiser. Seven torpedoes were fired at 4,500 yards but the tracks were seen by the enemy and she turned away.

destroyers, *Mary Rose* and *Strongbow* and two armed trawlers – a perfectly adequate force against U-boats but totally inadequate for the foe with which they would meet. On 17 October 1917, *Mary Rose* was leading the convoy and *Strongbow* was bringing up the rear. With fog reducing visibility to only 4,000yd, *Strongbow* sighted two fast ships coming up astern but took them for British light cruisers. They may well have been disguised with this in mind. The destroyer issued the challenge but did not go to action stations. *Brummer* closed to 3,000yd before opening up with a devastating fire, severing *Strongbow's* main steam pipe and disabling it. The destroyer went down with its colours flying and its after 4in gun still in action. At the same time the German ships jammed the British radio system so they could not summon help from Scapa Flow, which was only 65 miles distant. This was an early example of the use of electronic countermeasures. *Mary Rose* turned around and steamed towards the sound of gunfire, but before it could do anything it was sunk by a hail of fire from both the German ships. Having finished off the destroyers *Brummer* and *Bremse* sank nine of the transports, then disappeared back towards Germany. The German commanders were subsequently criticised for sinking neutral ships without giving the crews a chance to escape. The armed trawlers *Else* and *P. Fannon*, which had avoided the action, were able to return and pick up survivors. The first Beatty knew of the disaster was when the surviving merchantmen struggled back into port to tell their tale.

Mary Rose's conduct in the battle has been criticised. Some said that rather than engage such formidable opponents, the destroyer should have stood off, tried to draw the cruisers away from the merchantmen, and kept attempting to radio for help. This might have been the wiser course but the action the ship took was more typical of the aggressive spirit of destroyer commanders.

The Germans did not follow up this success as they wanted to preserve their major ships as potential bargaining counters in any forthcoming peace negotiations, however on 11 December 1917 eight large German destroyers mounted a further raid on the Scandinavian convoys. Four of the raiders fell upon some stragglers from a convoy and sank three ships, including an armed trawler. The other four German destroyers encountered a convoy of six merchantmen escorted by the destroyers *Partridge* and *Pellew* off Bergen. *Partridge* was quickly disabled and sunk, but it did manage to get a signal off which alerted a force of British light cruisers. It also had time to fire a torpedo which hit *V100* but failed to explode. *Pellew*, having sustained damage to the engine room, could do little to protect the merchantmen, which were all sunk, but it made good its escape into Norwegian territorial waters.

These two incidents greatly heartened German naval planners and obliged the Royal Navy to keep a force of heavy ships at sea to support the Scandinavian convoys. However, the Germans did not continue their aggressive tactics. The inaction and demoralisation of their fleet was one of the factors leading to the collapse of the Kaiser's regime. Possibly a more aggressive use of destroyers to supplement to U-boat campaign might have had a beneficial effect on naval morale.

CONCLUSION

The destroyers of the Royal Navy had an exciting and active war. Their role had evolved from acting as a deterrent to enemy torpedo-boats and carrying out occasional sneak attacks on capital ships, to forming a vital component of the battlefleet. Perhaps even more importantly, destroyers asserted themselves as a class of ship which could deliver command of the seas, inhibiting enemy maritime trade and protecting friendly merchantmen. The large number of these little ships built by both sides, in spite of the urgent demands placed on industry for other types of weapon, is a testament to their usefulness.

Having said this, actions such as Jutland and the earlier encounters at Heligoland Bight and the Dogger Bank did show that the extreme views about the future of capital ships expressed by the *Jeune École* were not correct. Sea-launched torpedoes were not to bring an end to the era of the big-gun warship, and destroyer attacks were not really effective against a well-designed and well-handled battlefleet. This was particularly disappointing for the Germans, who had held high hopes for their destroyer forces.

Destroyers made an important contribution to the development of the Royal Navy in another way. Destroyer officers and men, confined on a small ship with all the discomfort and difficulty attendant on such an environment, brought a new ethos to the service, emphasising the need for self-reliance and individual decision-making. In the "small-ship navy" there was no room for the formality and rigid class divisions which prevailed in other parts of the battlefleet. Relatively young and inexperienced officers found themselves in command of fast and heavily armed ships and often had to take vital tactical decisions themselves, instead of waiting to be told what to do by the flagship. If this ethos had been more prevalent in their seniors who commanded the great ships at Jutland, the outcome might have been a decisive victory for Britain. Significantly, the Navy which performed so superbly in World War II was to a large extent officered by men who had served in destroyers and were consequently far more self-reliant and less inhibited by "form" than their predecessors.

Not a good career move! *Violet* (C Class) aground on a sandbank. The vessel, which survived the incident, is apparently having non-essential gear jettisoned in order to lighten it.

INDEX

References to illustrations are shown in **bold**.